Jesus
and
Christianity

Alan Brown

HODDER
Wayland

an imprint of Hodder Children's Books

Great Religious Leaders

The Buddha and Buddhism
Guru Nanak and Sikhism
Krishna and Hinduism

Jesus and Christianity
Muhammad and Islam
Moses and Judaism

© White-Thomson Publishing Ltd 2002

Produced for Hodder Wayland by White-Thomson Publishing Ltd
2/3 St Andrew's Place, Lewes, E Sussex, BN7 1UP, UK

Editor: Margot Richardson   Graphics and maps: Tim Mayer
Designer: Jane Hawkins   Proofreader: Philippa Smith

First published in 2002 by Hodder Wayland, an imprint of Hodder Children's Books.

British Library Cataloguing in Publication Data
Brown, Alan, 1944-
   Jesus and Christianity. - (Great Religious Leaders)
   1. Jesus Christ 2. Christianity I. Title
   230
ISBN 0 7502 3702 3

Printed in Hong Kong

Hodder Children's Books
A division of Hodder Headline Limited
338 Euston Road, London NW1 3BH

Cover top: A Greek icon of Jesus
Cover main: A Roman Catholic church service
Title page: Holy week procession in Spain

Picture Acknowledgements: The publisher would like to thank the following for permission to reproduce their pictures:
AKG 4, 6, 7, 8, 9 (Cameraphoto), 10, 11 (Erich Lessing), 12 (S. Domingie), 13 (Cameraphoto), 15, 16, 17 (Cameraphoto), 18 (Erich Lessing), 19 (bottom) (Erich Lessing), 21 (Erich Lessing), 24 (Cameraphoto), 25, 26, 27 (top) (Cameraphoto), 29 (Erich Lessing); Art Directors and Trip Photo Library cover top, 34 (T. Bognar), 40 (H. Rogers), 41 (D. Butcher), 45 (top) P. Treanor, 45 (bottom) D. Butcher; Bridgeman Art Library 14 (Brooklyn Museum of Art), 19 (top) (Brooklyn Museum of Art), 20 (Brooklyn Museum of Art), 22 (Biblioteca Estense, Modena); Britstock-IFA 28 (Gerig), 31 (Braun), 33; Circa Photo Library cover main; Eye Ubiquitous 1 (Brian Harding), 5 (David Cumming), 23 (Bruce Adams), 32 (Adina Tovy Amsel), 35 (bottom) (David Cumming), 36 (David Cumming), 38 (top) (Skjold); Hodder Wayland Picture Library 27 (bottom) (Jim Holmes), 39, 44; Impact Photos 37 (Christophe Bluntzer); James Davis Travel Photography 30, 38 (bottom); ; Popperfoto/Reuters 35 (top); South American Pictures 43 (Hilary Bradt); Ole Buntzen/POLFOTO 42.

Contents

What is Christianity?

Everyone who calls himself or herself a Christian believes in the person of Jesus Christ.

▲ No one knows what Jesus really looked like as he lived too long ago. This image was painted in the twelfth century CE.

Jesus was born about 2,000 years ago in Bethlehem, in present-day Palestine. His family and all the people he lived among were Jewish. He moved with Mary, his mother, and Joseph, her husband, to Nazareth in the north of present-day Israel where he grew up. When he was about thirty years old he began to teach. His message was that people should believe in and obey God. They should accept God as ruler and that they were part of God's 'kingdom'. If the people listened to Jesus and believed what he said they would be in a close and special relationship with God.

Jesus became very popular and drew large crowds which worried the authorities. Some religious leaders also felt that Jesus was saying things about himself that made it appear that he was God. This was called blasphemy and the Jewish leaders did not like it. They, together with Pontius Pilate, the Roman governor of Israel, arrested Jesus. He was tried and executed.

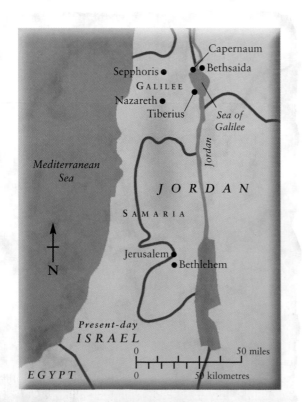

◀ Jesus spent most of his life in Galilee.

Christians believe Jesus rose from the dead. He met his followers, talking and eating with them. Finally, he was taken into heaven.

In the years after his death, Jesus' teaching spread. It moved out of Israel, into the lands conquered by the Roman Empire, into North Africa and beyond. People who were not Jews – Gentiles – and knew nothing of Jewish thinking became followers. They became Christians. Christians are people who believe and trust in God and in Jesus Christ, in what he did for them and in the message he brought.

Russian women hold icons (religious pictures) at an outdoor church service. ▼

CHRIST AND 'THE WAY'

The word 'Christ' comes from a Greek word Christos, which means 'anointed'. People such as priests or kings were sometimes anointed with oil in a special ceremony that made them a leader. Christians believe that Jesus was chosen to be their king and leader. The Jewish word for anointed is 'Messiah', and Jesus is often called Messiah as well.

Christianity was first known as 'The Way' because Jesus taught his disciples 'the way' to God. It wasn't called Christianity (followers of Jesus Christ) for nearly a hundred years after his death.

The Life of Jesus

Jesus is Born

A woman called Mary was visited by the angel Gabriel, a messenger from God. Gabriel told Mary that she would have a son, to be called Jesus. Christians believe that the Spirit of God had somehow created the baby in Mary's womb. At the time, Mary was engaged to Joseph, a carpenter. Just before Jesus was due to be born, Mary and Joseph had to go on a long journey to Bethlehem, to take part in a census.

When Mary and Joseph arrived in Bethlehem they could not find anywhere to stay, but eventually an innkeeper allowed them to sleep in his stable. There, among the animals, Jesus was born. Angels appeared to shepherds in the fields and told them the good news of this great birth. The shepherds decided to visit the new family in the stable.

The Bible (the Christian holy book) also tells of a visit by some wise men from the East, called Magi. When they were trying to find Jesus they asked a king called Herod for help. Herod could tell them where Jesus was, but he asked them to return after they had found Jesus. He said he wanted to worship Jesus too, but Herod really wanted to kill him: he did not want competition from another 'king' of the Jews.

When Jesus was eight days old he was taken to the Jewish Temple (see page 30) where his parents gave thanks for his birth. There, they met two elderly religious

▲ Mary gave birth to Jesus in a stable. In old paintings, like this, holy people were often shown with a halo, or ring of light, around their heads.

people, Simeon and Anna, who told them that Jesus was indeed a very special baby.

Both the Magi and Mary and Joseph were warned in dreams that Herod wanted to harm Jesus. The Magi did not return to Herod and Joseph, Mary and Jesus fled into Egypt.

Later, when it was safe to return, Mary and Joseph took Jesus to Nazareth. There, he grew up, probably learning to be a carpenter, like Joseph.

SIMEON AND ANNA

Simeon was an old man, but God had told him that he would not die until he had seen the Messiah. When Mary and Joseph brought Jesus to the Temple Simeon took the baby in his arms, praised God, and said that now he had seen Jesus he could die in peace. Joseph and Mary were surprised at Simeon's words.

Anna was a woman who worshipped in the Temple, night and day, often going without eating. She also saw Jesus, believed he was the Messiah, and told many people about him.

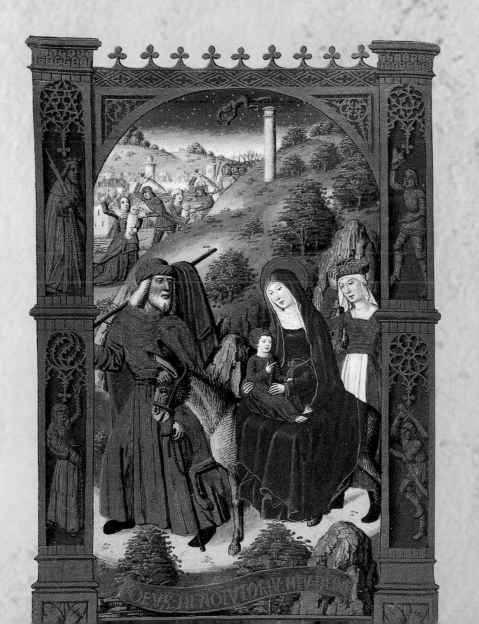

◀ When Herod found out that the wise men had tricked him he ordered his men to kill all the children who lived in or near Bethlehem and were two years old and under.

Jesus' Teaching Begins

Nothing is known of Jesus' life from the age of twelve until he began to teach and travel around the country, probably in his early thirties. He was baptized by his cousin, John the Baptist. As Jesus emerged from the water, he saw the Spirit of God come down on him, like a dove, and a voice from heaven said, 'This is my own dear Son, with whom I am well pleased'.

Jesus went into the desert for forty days to think how best he could do what God wanted. He was tempted three times by the devil: to change stones into bread; to throw himself off the highest point of the Temple in Jerusalem (see page 30); and to bow down and worship the devil in exchange for the kingdoms of the world. Jesus rejected all these, and left the desert to begin his work.

When Jesus went into the desert he did not eat for forty days or nights. In those days Jewish people went without eating twice a week to concentrate more deeply on God. ▼

When Jesus chose fishermen as his disciples he told them, 'I will teach you to become fishers of people instead of fish.'

Jesus gathered twelve followers, or disciples, to join him. First Jesus called Simon (later called Peter) and his brother Andrew, who were fishermen, then two others, James and John. More followed soon after.

When Jesus started teaching he wanted people to think. He wanted people to stop, listen and then understand what he was saying. Jesus wanted people to know that God loved them and cared for them. He healed people who were sick, and he even raised people from the dead. These acts are called miracles.

News of this new teacher spread and people came from far and wide to hear him. However, Jesus did not always agree with the teaching of the religious authorities so he made some powerful enemies.

REJECTED BY HIS HOME TOWN

There were many healers and miracle workers around at the time of Jesus. He would have been one among many. When Jesus started to teach in Nazareth the local people took offence at him. They had watched him grow up and probably found it hard to believe that he was a special person. Jesus did not perform many healings there because of the people's lack of faith.

He ... 'went to his home town. He taught in their meeting place, and the people were so amazed that they asked, "Where does he get all this wisdom and the power to perform these miracles? Isn't he the son of the carpenter? Isn't Mary his mother, and aren't James, Joseph, Simon and Judas his brothers? Don't his sisters still live here in our town? How can he do all this?" '

Matthew 13: 54–56

▲ The Passover meal that Jesus shared with his disciples became known as The Last Supper. Judas, the disciple who betrayed Jesus, can be seen on the far right (with red hair). He is holding a bag of silver coins that he was paid for his information.

The Last Week

Jesus' ministry lasted for three years. He travelled through Israel making both friends and enemies. On the Sunday before his death he entered Jerusalem humbly riding on a donkey. This symbolized his message of peace. Crowds threw palm branches (symbols of victory) in his path and shouted, 'Praise God! God bless him who comes in the name of the Lord!'

During the next week, Jesus taught his disciples about difficult times that were to come. At the end of the week they all gathered together in a room to celebrate the Jewish festival of Passover. During the meal, Jesus told them that one of the disciples would betray him to his enemies. He also said that Peter would disown him three times before the cock crowed the next morning. As they were eating, Jesus broke some bread and shared wine from a cup. He told his disciples that when they ate together they should break bread and drink wine as a way of remembering him.

After the meal Jesus and his disciples went to the Garden of Gethsemane. Jesus prayed for courage to carry out God's will. Soon Judas arrived with guards who arrested Jesus and took him away.

Jesus was tried by the priests and elders who decided that he should be killed. They handed him over to Pontius Pilate, the Roman governor. They all believed he was a troublemaker stirring up the people. As Jesus was appearing before Pilate, Peter was challenged three times about his friendship with Jesus. Each time he denied all knowledge of Jesus because he was afraid – and then the cock crowed.

Pilate examined the evidence against Jesus, then handed him over to his soldiers to be killed. Jesus was crucified – nailed to a wooden cross – with a criminal on either side of him. Darkness came over the land for three hours. At his death he cried out, 'My God, my God, why have you forsaken me?'

After Jesus' death, his body was taken down with care, dressed for burial and placed in a tomb. A large stone was rolled over the entrance to seal it.

Crucifixion was the way the Romans executed criminals, slaves and foreigners. The crucified person died because he could not breathe, so dying could take a long time. ▼

Jesus Rises from the Dead

When the women saw the angel at the tomb they were terrified, but he reminded them that Jesus had foretold how he would rise from the dead.

Jesus was crucified on a Friday. The next day was the Jewish Sabbath. When a small group of women, including Mary, his mother, came to the tomb on the following Sunday they were amazed to see that the stone had been rolled back. Entering the tomb, the women were told by an angel that Jesus had risen from the dead. They ran away, terrified, and told the disciples, but they were not believed until Peter went into the tomb, saw it was empty and found the cloth that had been wrapped around Jesus' body.

Some time later, two of Jesus' followers were walking along a road and met a stranger. They told him about the events in Jerusalem. The stranger reminded them how the Jewish scriptures pointed to the death of Jesus and his rising from the dead – the resurrection. When they arrived at an inn they invited the stranger to join them in a meal. As he broke the bread at the meal they recognized him as Jesus and he disappeared. The two rushed back to Jerusalem to tell the disciples.

Jesus appeared a number of times to his disciples. One of these was Thomas, who had not been present when Jesus first appeared to the others. Jesus invited Thomas to touch the wounds on his hands, feet and side and Thomas believed immediately that Jesus was alive again. Jesus appeared to Peter and others while they were fishing, and ate with them. Each time Jesus appeared he confirmed the disciples' belief that he really had risen from the dead.

Several weeks after Jesus appeared to his disciples he was taken into heaven. He left them with the promise that the Holy Spirit would guide them in the future.

HOLY TRINITY

Christians believe in one God. There has only ever been one God, and as God does not change so there will only ever be one God. They refer to God in three ways: as the Father and creator; as the Son, Jesus Christ; and as the Holy Spirit, the power of God in people's lives. Christians believe they understand God better when they believe in these three aspects of God.

◀ Thomas would not believe Jesus was alive unless he could touch Jesus' wounds. The expression 'Doubting Thomas' has passed into the English language, describing someone who is hard to convince.

The Teachings of Jesus

Jesus' most important message was that all people should not only believe in God but should worship Him and, above all, try to do what God wants for their lives. Jesus described anyone who did this as belonging to the 'Kingdom of God' or the 'Kingdom of Heaven'.

▲ Such large crowds started to follow Jesus that he could not talk to them inside a building. A mountainside was the ideal place for them to both see and hear him.

Sermon on the Mount

One of the main collections of Jesus' teaching is now called the Sermon on the Mount. It summarizes much of what he taught. Jesus had been travelling all over Galilee, teaching in Jewish meeting places and healing every kind of disease and sickness. News about him had spread all over the country and a huge crowd of people had gathered. Many of these people wanted to be cured of their illnesses. When Jesus saw the crowd, he climbed up the side of a mountain and began to teach.

His message was about how people should live, and how their thoughts and actions would affect their relationship with God. He taught that you should love your enemies, not judge other people, and forgive them for wrong-doing. You should go out of your way to put other people's needs before your own, however hard this might be. Jesus was also concerned for the poor and the outcasts of society.

▲ People were surprised at Jesus' teaching for he spoke with such power because his authority came from God.

Jesus told people that it was very difficult for rich people to enter the kingdom of heaven because the more money people have, the easier it is just to think about themselves.

He went on to explain that people should not even worry about practical things such as having enough to eat, drink or wear but to concentrate more on God. His strongest words were against hypocrites, especially religious ones, and those who showed off how 'good' they were.

THE SERMON ON THE MOUNT

'God blesses those people who depend only on him.
They belong to the kingdom of heaven! …
God blesses those people who are humble.
The earth will belong to them! …
God blesses those people who are merciful.
They will be treated with mercy! …
God blesses those people who are treated badly for doing right.
They belong to the kingdom of heaven.'

Matthew 5: 3, 5, 7, 10

Teaching through Parables

Houses on rock and sand

Jesus finished the Sermon on the Mount by telling a story, called a parable, about two houses, one built on rock and the other on sand. If a house is built on sand then there will be no firm foundation. When the wind, rain and floods come, the house will crash down. But if a house is built on rock it will not fall. Jesus said that anyone who doesn't obey his teachings is like a foolish person who builds a house on sand. Anyone who obeys his teaching is like a wise person who builds a house on solid rock and will always be safe.

Word pictures

A parable is a story that has one or more meanings and paints a 'word picture'. Jesus was a very clever storyteller and often used parables to try to help people understand his message. Parables are meant to help people think, because they will remember the story long after they first heard it.

The Good Samaritan helps the injured man by the side of the road. By using an unpopular Samaritan in his story, Jesus was making people rethink the way they viewed other people. ▼

The Good Samaritan

One of the best-known parables tells of a Jewish man who went on a journey. He was beaten up by robbers and left for dead. Some Jewish people walked by, including some religious people, but they left him lying by the side of the road. It was only when a man from Samaria came to his aid that the man was saved. The Samaritan took him to an inn and paid for him to be looked after. The Jews hated the

Samaritans, so this is an example of an outcast helping when others passed by. Jesus asked a question: 'Who was a neighbour to this man?'

Forgiveness

The parables are also about forgiveness, the rule of God and that God guides those who understand Jesus' teaching.

Another parable is about a man with two sons. The younger son asked for his half of his father's money, went away, and soon spent it all in wild living. He ended up living among pigs with nothing to eat. He decided to go home, beg his father to forgive him and ask to be treated as a slave. The elder brother was furious, but the father said, 'He was lost and has now been found.' Because the younger son was really sorry for what he had done, his father forgave him and celebrated his return. This parable shows that God forgives people who are truly sorry for wrong things they have done.

This sixteenth-century painting shows the father forgiving his son. Forgiveness is one of the most important parts of Jesus' teaching. ▼

Miracles

Jesus performed miracles to help people understand his teaching. His healing miracles were meant to challenge people, just like his teaching. Deaf and blind people were healed, not just because he felt sorry for them, but to make the people (and those who were watching) see, hear and understand his message.

One man who could not walk was brought to see Jesus in a house. The crush was so great his friends could not carry him through the door. Instead, they climbed up

▲ As well as healing the sick, Jesus raised people from the dead. A man called Lazarus had been dead for four days when Jesus brought him back to life.

HEALING THE SICK

Most of Jesus' miracles were to do with healing people who were ill. People often believed that illness was caused by 'sin' or wrongdoing; they felt guilty and became ill. The miracles were signs of Jesus' – and God's – power and authority. By healing people Jesus forgave their sins. This made some of the religious leaders very angry. They believed that only God could forgive sins, and they did not believe that Jesus was the Son of God.

In the time of Jesus, most houses had flat roofs, covered with tiles. To lower the man down, his friends would have removed some tiles to make a hole. ▶

on the roof of the room where Jesus was teaching, and lowered the man down through a hole. Jesus told the man to take up his bed and walk because his sins were forgiven. The man got up, walked out and went on his way rejoicing.

Feeding the 5,000

Miracles were also a demonstration of God's power.

There is a story of Jesus feeding 5,000 people. Jesus had been teaching them; the day passed and they all became hungry. His disciples asked Jesus how they could feed so many people. One disciple brought forward a young boy who had five loaves and two fishes. Jesus divided the loaves and fishes between all the people and after everyone had eaten there was so much food left over it filled twelve baskets.

Miracles, as Jesus used them, were living pictures and a way of teaching by using real life events.

Feeding the 5,000 was one way that Jesus showed how God takes care of people who believe in Jesus and his teaching. ▶

Making people think

Jesus' style of teaching was to challenge people. He wanted to make them think about God and the way they lived. He used vivid images to help people understand:

'It's easier for a camel to go through the eye of a needle than for a rich person to get into God's kingdom.'

Matthew 19:24

At times, Jesus annoyed some important religious Jews, such as the Pharisees, by being too casual about Jewish religious rules. For example, he was more relaxed about what was permitted on the Sabbath (the Jewish holy day of rest). However, he said:

'Don't suppose that I came to do away with the Law and the Prophets. I did not come to do away with them, but to give them their full meaning.'

Matthew 5:17

Groups of Pharisees (shown standing to the right of the picture) often argued with Jesus. ▼

THE PHARISEES

Pharisees were members of a Jewish sect, and some became Jesus' most fierce opponents. They followed Jewish customs and laws very closely. As religious teachers, they had a responsibility to set a good example. However Jesus said that the details were not always that important.

Some Pharisees were angered by what Jesus said or did, and often tried to question or argue with him. Jesus condemned some of them as hypocrites: that although they pretended to be holy they said one thing and did another.

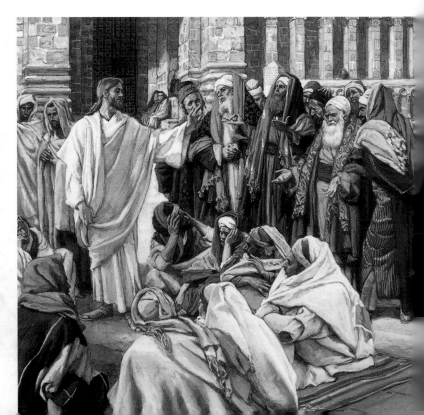

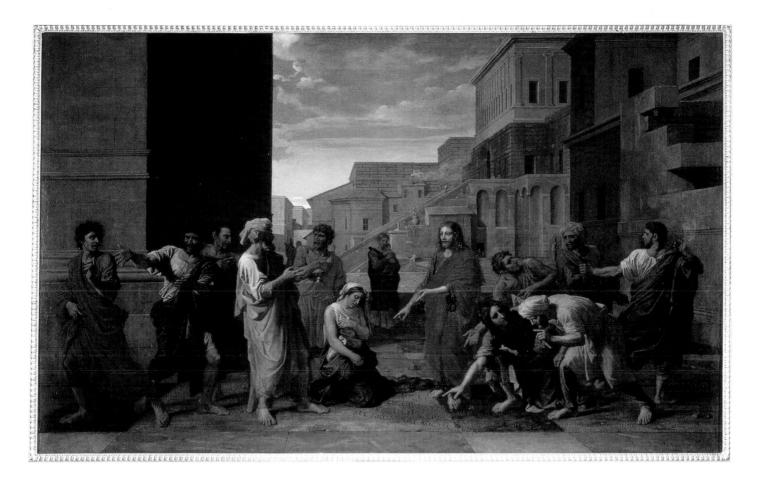

Rules and laws

Jesus taught people that it was important to find out what God wanted and then to do it. He wanted people to think first about God and then each other's needs. Rules and laws were necessary but rules should not get in the way. Love for God should come first and then love for each other.

There is a story (to do with rules) of a woman who was caught being unfaithful to her husband. She was brought to Jesus with the question, 'What should happen to her? She is guilty and under the Law the penalty is death by stoning.' Jesus said, 'If any of you have never sinned, then go ahead and throw the first stone at her.' His opponents melted away and he told the woman not to do wrong again.

▲ Jesus used the example of the woman who had sinned to make a point: everyone has done things that are wrong and we should not judge other people. Only God can judge.

The Sacred Texts

The Christian Bible is divided into two parts, called the Old Testament and the New Testament. The word testament means 'promise', so the two testaments are the story of God's promises to the world.

▲ Before printing was invented, Bibles were written out by hand, and were often beautifully decorated. This Italian Bible was made in the fifteenth century.

There are so many different books in the Bible it is often called a library. They include poetry, history, rules, letters and stories. The Bible was written by many different people over hundreds of years. The final collection of books was not agreed until 397 CE.

The Old Testament

This is the first part of the Bible. It includes the Jewish scripture known as the Torah. It describes how God created the world, and the lives and deeds of the early prophets. It was originally written in Hebrew.

The New Testament

The second part of the Bible was written in Greek, probably between 65 and 125 CE. It tells of the life of Jesus and how people should live according to his teaching. Christians believe the New Testament shows how the coming of Jesus and the importance of his life was foretold in the Old Testament. Jesus brought a new way of living so the story of his life is called the 'New' Testament.

▲ An Orthodox priest (see page 35) reads a Bible passage to worshippers in Bethlehem.

The word of God

The Bible is treated with great reverence, read with devotion and studied carefully by all Christians. It is used in most church services because Christians believe it is inspired by God. Some believe that everything in the Bible is factually true; others believe it uses stories and symbols to tell of God's love for the world.

A POPULAR BOOK

The Bible is the world's best-selling book. It has been translated into every known written language. In the UK, the old King James version of the Bible, published in 1611 CE, has had a great influence on the language. Many phrases from it are in regular use today.

The Gospels

The four Gospels form the first part of the New Testament. The word 'Gospel' means 'good news'. The gospels were written to bring the 'good news' of Jesus' life, death and resurrection to the world. The Gospels were written by four different people: Matthew, Mark, Luke and John. Little is known about the authors, although Matthew and John are traditionally believed to have been disciples of Jesus.

Different views

Each Gospel has a different emphasis and gives a different view of Jesus. They do, however, follow the same basic story. The Gospels are not detailed stories of Jesus' life but they are collections of sayings and events woven together to create an impression of who Jesus was and what he did. Many people believe the four Gospels because they were probably written between thirty and a hundred years after Jesus' death. The authors might have been able to meet and listen to Jesus' followers.

Only Matthew and Luke tell about Jesus' birth. Their stories are very different, and only agree on the names of Jesus and his parents; where Jesus was born; that Mary was a virgin and that the family went to live in Nazareth.

Otherwise, the Gospels of Matthew, Mark and Luke are very similar. John contains stories and teaching that are

▲ The gospel writer Matthew, pictured in the fourteenth century. Matthew is sometimes called 'the evangelist', as he wrote down the 'good news' of Jesus' life and teaching.

not in the other Gospels, providing a very different approach to Jesus' life. There are no parables, and the order of events is different. Jesus makes long speeches about himself and most of the miracles are different too.

Jesus is a powerful figure in Mark's Gospel and was often in conflict with religious leaders. Mark showed Jesus as having a sense of urgency; he wanted to spread God's message quickly.

Matthew shows Jesus to be the Teacher of Israel, and Jesus' followers are commanded to go out and teach all nations, not just the Jews.

Luke describes how Jesus taught that every person can be saved. Jesus cares for the poor and those who suffer. Luke also shows the important role women played in the life of Jesus.

A Russian painting of John with his symbol, the eagle. It dates from the eighteenth or nineteenth century, so the artist did not know what John actually looked like. ▼

SYMBOLS OF THE GOSPEL WRITERS

Each of the four Gospel writers has a symbol that was often used to identify them. Matthew's symbol is the human face; Mark's is a roaring lion; Luke's is an ox; and John's is an eagle.

These symbols are usually used in Christian art and can be seen in church decorations, paintings or in stained glass windows.

Paul and the Epistles

Paul was originally called Saul. He had trained as a Pharisee and had persecuted the followers of Jesus. After he became a Christian he took the name of Paul and spent the rest of his life teaching about Jesus. He travelled far and wide near the Mediterranean, encouraging people to be strong in their Christian faith.

Epistles

Paul's letters, called Epistles, are the earliest written records of Jesus' life. He visited many places where Christians had begun to gather together. No one really knows exactly what he wrote, but there are letters in his name to the churches in Rome, Corinth, Galatia, Philippi, Colossae and Thessalonica, and to people called Timothy, Titus and Philemon. Paul probably died in Rome in 60–65 CE.

▲ Paul's letters form a large part of the New Testament.

Explaining Jesus' life

Paul wrote that by rising from the dead, Jesus had been taken up into heaven and would come to earth again bringing God's rule, a time of justice and peace. The resurrection was proof that Jesus was the Son of God.

Paul believed the awful death of Jesus shows how powerfully God loves all people. Christians believe that on

▲ This Italian painting shows the disciple Peter (right) and Paul (left). Peter (see page 34) and Paul played major roles in shaping Christianity in its early years.

FAITH, HOPE AND LOVE

Paul believed that the three most important parts of Christianity were
- faith: in Jesus
- hope: in the promise of eternal life offered by Jesus, and
- love: given freely, without the need for reward.

Paul said that the greatest of the three is unselfish Christian love.

▲ Belief in Jesus is the most important part of Christianity.

the cross Jesus paid for (atoned) the sin of Adam. (In the Bible, Adam, the first man, broke God's law and had to leave the Garden of Eden.) In his letters, Paul compared Jesus with Adam. Jesus, on the other hand, obeyed God completely. He therefore mended the relationship between God and people that Adam had broken.

Great Sayings and Favourite Texts

The most famous and most used Christian prayer is The Lord's Prayer. Jesus' disciples asked him for guidance on how they should pray. Jesus gave them a simple prayer using 'Father' to address God. Sometimes called 'Our Father' after the first two words, it is used by all Christians throughout the world.

> *'Our Father in heaven, help us to honour your name.*
> *Come and set up your kingdom,*
> *So that everyone on earth will obey you, as you are*
> *obeyed in heaven.*
> *Give us our food for today.*
> *Forgive us for doing wrong, as we forgive others.*
> *Keep us from being tempted and protect us from evil.'*
>
> Matthew 6:9–13

People talk to God, or pray, quietly by themselves or at church services. They often kneel to pray, or stand, as in this church. ▼

Another favourite text is John 3:16:

> *'God loved the people of this world so much that he gave his only Son, so that everyone who has faith in him will have eternal life and never really die.'*

This verse says in a few words what Christians believe about God's love for the whole world: everyone who accepts Jesus will live forever.

The words of Jesus

Jesus summed up the whole of the Jewish Law (Torah) in a few words. This was a typical style of Jewish teaching and similar teaching can be found in the Old Testament as well as in the Jewish teaching around the time of Jesus. Hillel, a great teacher who lived just before Jesus, said, *'What is hateful to you, do not do to your neighbour. That is the whole Torah. The rest is commentary.'*

The Bible sums up this most important part of both the Jewish and the Christian faith:

> *'Love the Lord your God with all your heart, soul, strength and mind. ...*
>   *Love your neighbours as much as you love yourself.'*
>   Luke 10:27

Favourite parts of the Bible

Many Christians will have favourite Bible passages that they read regularly. There will also be passages they read for support, for comfort, to give thanks, or just to feel they are close to the words they believe Jesus spoke.

Hundreds of years ago, many people could not read, so the stories of the Bible were shown in paintings or, in Europe, in stained glass windows. This window shows the birth of Jesus (bottom) and the visit of the Magi (top). ▼

The Sacred Places

Jerusalem

Jerusalem is a sacred place for Christians because it is the city where Jesus was crucified and where he rose from the dead.

During the three years Jesus travelled around teaching, his goal was to enter Jerusalem on his final journey because it was the centre of the Jewish world. It is not certain how many people lived in Jerusalem at the time of Jesus. One estimate is 30,000, but the number at major festival times may have risen to 120,000.

◀ Parts of the old town in Jerusalem have hardly changed since the time of Jesus.

Jerusalem has been the centre of the Jewish religion for 3,000 years. King David, Jesus' ancestor, made it his capital city and Solomon, David's son, built the first Temple there. The Temple had been destroyed centuries earlier and in Jesus' time it was newly rebuilt. The Temple was destroyed again in 70 CE by the Romans. Today only its western wall still stands. This is a very holy place for Jews and many come to pray at the wall.

Jerusalem is also a sacred city for Muslims as events that are important to them happened there.

There is a story in the Gospels of Jesus driving out traders and money-changers from the Temple. At the time, Jews came to the Temple to give thanks to God by sacrificing birds, sheep and goats. The traders in the Temple courtyards sold these animals. However Jesus accused them of turning the Temple into a place of robbers.

Easter

At Easter (see page 36), Christians come to Jerusalem in their thousands from all over the world to remember the last week of Jesus' life. On Good Friday pilgrims follow the route Jesus took to his crucifixion; called the Via Dolorosa (Road of Sorrows). Pilgrims carry crosses, sharing again in Jesus' final journey to his death.

A sepulchre is a small room where a dead person is laid or buried. The Church of the Holy Sepulchre is richly decorated to honour a very sacred place. ▼

Church of the Holy Sepulchre

One of the most visited places in Jerusalem is the Church of the Holy Sepulchre which some believe is built on the spot where Jesus was buried. There has been a church there for 1,700 years. Pilgrims come to pray, to feel they are close to Jesus. He was almost certainly not buried there, but Christians want a place where they can focus their minds on Jesus.

Galilee

Galilee, in the north of present-day Israel, was the setting for much of Jesus' teaching. The Gospels tell of Jesus teaching in the open air and in the synagogue at Capernaum and, of course, he was brought up in Nazareth. He appears to have avoided the main towns of Tiberius and Sepphoris. It may have been because the king who ruled there, Herod, was the person who executed John the Baptist, Jesus' cousin.

Today's farms and buildings now cover the land around the Sea of Galilee where Jesus once walked. ▼

Modern fishermen still fish on the Sea of Galilee, nearly 2,000 years after Jesus' disciples. ▶

Galilee's population was mixed: there were Jews and non-Jews. In the Bible, Galilee is described as 'Galilee of the Nations' to show the mix of nationalities living there. It was separated from the south by Samaria. Jewish travellers going south to Jerusalem would either have to make a detour to avoid the country, or pass through it, anxious for their safety because of the conflict between Jews and Samaritans.

Galilee's most outstanding feature is the Sea of Galilee. It has various names – Lake Tiberias, Lake Gennesaret – and is rich in fish. Bethsaida, one of the villages on its shores, is often mentioned in the Gospels. It means 'House of Fishing' and three of Jesus' disciples came from the village. Some of his disciples, including Peter and John, were fishermen. Jesus did, in fact, curse the people of Bethsaida for failing to respond to the miracles he performed there.

For many pilgrims, moving around the sites in Galilee enables them to capture the flavour of life at the time of Jesus. Buildings change, towns and villages rise and fall but the landscape is the same. Boats still fish on the lake and it is not hard to imagine it in the time of Jesus: to sit on the lake in the silence of dawn is to travel back down the centuries.

GALILEE

Galilee simply means 'district', or 'circle'. Galilee stood at the crossroads of the trading world at the time of Jesus. Camel trains carrying goods moved across the region. People from many lands visited and settled, bringing their own customs and languages. Galileans were easily identified by their regional accent. They were considered to be a troublesome people. The Pharisees thought Galileans were rather relaxed in the way they followed the Jewish law.

Rome

Rome, often called 'The Eternal City' because of its age and importance over thousands of years, holds a unique place in Christian history. It was the centre of the Mediterranean area and the European world at the time of Jesus. It is a special place for many Christians.

It is likely that Peter, Jesus' disciple and choice as the 'rock' on which the Church would be built, went to Rome and was killed there. Tradition says he was crucified upside down because he felt he was not worthy to die in the same way as Jesus. Paul (see page 26) was taken to Rome for trial and was probably executed there too.

▲ St Peter's Church in Rome is believed to be where the remains of Peter are buried.

The Romans persecuted Christians for 250 years. Many Christians were persecuted in Rome; they had to worship secretly in underground burial places called catacombs. Once the Emperor Constantine became a Christian, in the early fourth century CE, Rome became the centre of the Christian world and saw itself as more important than other Christian cities.

Bishop of Rome

Peter is referred to as the first Bishop of Rome and today the head of the Roman Catholic Church, the Pope, takes the title 'Bishop of Rome'. Half the world's Christians are Roman Catholic so Rome has a special place in their hearts. The Pope lives in Vatican City, a state within the city of Rome. Pilgrims come from all over the world to visit St Peter's Church and to worship.

The Pope blesses the crowd from the top of St Peter's after calling for peace in the world's trouble spots. ▶

The Russian Orthodox leader, called the Patriarch, holding an outdoor church service. ▼

FAMILY DIFFERENCES

Christianity became the official religion of the Roman Empire in the late fourth century. The Bishop of Rome had already begun to claim that he was the senior leader, but the Churches in the east of the empire did not accept this. They also believed they kept to the true or 'orthodox' way and did not accept changes Rome wished to make. The Churches of the Middle East, including Greece and Russia, split from the Western Church in 1054 CE, and are now known as Orthodox Churches. Today, the Roman Catholic and Orthodox Churches worship in different ways and even have a different calendar of festivals.

The last main group of Christians are called Protestants. The Protestant Church split from the Roman Catholics in Europe during the sixteenth century.

Festivals and Celebrations

Christian festivals are usually marked by special church services and, in some places, parades through the streets.

▲ A Good Friday parade in Kerala, India, re-enacting how Jesus carried the cross to the place where he was crucified.

Easter

The events in the Christian year that are centred around Easter are the most important ones for Christians. Easter marks the death and resurrection of Jesus.

Lent

The period begins with Lent, forty days of preparation for Easter. Lent starts on Ash Wednesday when crosses, made from palm leaves, are burned and the ashes are smeared on to Christians' foreheads to show they are sorry for their sins. Many Christians want to share in Jesus' temptation in the desert by giving up something they really like for forty days (such as chocolate) and carrying out extra Bible study.

Palm Sunday

Palm Sunday falls on the Sunday before Easter. It recalls the entry of Jesus into Jerusalem, riding on a donkey, when crowds threw palm branches in his path. Today, palm leaves or branches are handed out to church-goers.

Holy Week

The week before Easter is called Holy Week. There are extra services in churches and the story of the last week of Jesus' life is read. Christians try to share in the pain and suffering of Jesus. The Thursday is known as Maundy Thursday.

On this day, Jesus had washed the feet of his disciples. This is often re-enacted in churches.

Good Friday

Good Friday marks the day when Jesus was killed. (It is called 'Good' because Jesus' death was a 'good' act.) Christians often spend three hours in prayer, because when Jesus was on the cross there was darkness from the sixth to the ninth hour. Processions are held with Christians carrying a cross as Jesus would have done on his way to the crucifixion. Altars in many churches are stripped bare and all Christians remember it as a solemn, holy day.

Easter Day

Easter Eve (Saturday) is a day of watchfulness, waiting and prayer and many Christians spend the night awake watching for dawn to come. Easter Day begins as soon as dawn breaks. Christians throughout the world celebrate the resurrection of Jesus with joyful services.

Greek women create an Easter garden with flowers to celebrate Easter Day. ▼

During Advent, some Christians light four candles to mark the four Sundays leading up to Christmas.

The nativity scene, where Jesus is in the manger surrounded by his parents, shepherds and animals, is believed to have been started by Francis of Assisi, who lived in the thirteenth century. ▼

Christmas

Advent

The Christian year begins on the first Sunday in Advent (which means 'coming'), four weeks before Christmas. Advent is a period of preparation. Like Lent, it is a solemn time when Christians remember their faults and review their lives.

Jesus' birth

No one really knows when Jesus was born. The date is normally given as between 6 and 4 BCE as King Herod, who tried to kill the infant Jesus, died in 4 CE. In the fourth century, 25 December became accepted as the day to celebrate Jesus' birth. The Roman Emperor, Constantine, decided that the mid-winter festival of the Unconquered Sun, a Roman festival, should be used. Before then Jesus' birth was not celebrated at all.

The first church services start late on Christmas Eve, finishing on Christmas morning so Christians can celebrate the birth of Jesus as soon as possible. There are also many church services on Christmas Day itself.

Epiphany

January 6 is traditionally the time when the Magi, who were Gentiles, visited Jesus and is when he was shown to the world. It is also celebrated as the date when, many years later, Jesus was baptized by John the Baptist at the start of his ministry.

CHRISTMAS TRADITIONS

The nativity scene, the nativity play and giving names to the (Melchior, Balthazar and Caspar), as well as the giving of presents and decorating Christmas trees, have all added to the Bible story.

The birth of Jesus has become linked with the story of Saint Nicholas (Santa Klaus) who was supposed to bring presents for good children on 6 December.

▲ A Christmas parade with a man dressed up as Saint Nicholas.

Candlemas

The Christmas cycle ends on 2 February with Candlemas, when Jesus was brought to the Temple by Mary and Joseph to give thanks for his birth (see page 7). Jesus was declared by Simeon to be a 'Light to lighten the Gentiles and to bring glory to the people of Israel'; hence the title Candlemas.

Festival dates

Some Christians celebrate Christmas twelve days later than 25 December because of a change in the days of the calendar in the eighteenth century. Customs in the Orthodox Churches vary but many still celebrate Christmas on 7 January. Many Orthodox festivals, including Easter, therefore occur later than in the Western Churches.

Pentecost

During his life, Jesus promised his disciples that God would send the Holy Spirit (see page 13) to guide and support them.

After Jesus ascended into heaven the disciples gathered together to celebrate the Jewish festival of Shavuot. The Acts of the Apostles (one of the books of the New Testament, written by the Gospel writer Luke) tells the story of what happened. When the disciples were gathered together in one room,

'Suddenly there was a noise from heaven like the sound of a mighty wind! It filled the house where they were meeting. Then they saw what looked liked fiery tongues moving in all directions ...'

Acts of the Apostles 2:2–3

They were filled with the Holy Spirit and began to talk in many languages.

The word for 'spirit' in the Bible has a wide variety of meanings. It can mean 'breath' or 'life' and is the word used to describe what God breathed into Adam in the story of creation. The elements of wind and fire gave the disciples the power of the Holy Spirit.

Pentecost comes from a Greek word meaning 'fifty days'. It is celebrated on the seventh Sunday after Easter. In the UK, another name for Pentecost is

◄ Banners showing flames and fire adorn a church for the festival of Pentecost.

'Whitsun' (or White Sunday) because new Christians joined the church on that day and wore white clothes.

Pentecost is often seen to be the birthday of the Christian Church. Jesus had gone to heaven and the disciples were left to teach and preach. Jesus' life, death and resurrection had taught his disciples who he was and what his message was; now his followers had to go out, facing many hardships, to teach that message to the world. The coming of the Holy Spirit gave them the power, authority and courage to carry out the task.

THE PENTECOSTAL MOVEMENT

One of the fastest growing groups in Christianity in the last century has been the Pentecostal movement. It began in the USA over a hundred years ago and took its name from the feast of Pentecost. Its members believe in the power of the Holy Spirit and emphasize preaching and healing as ways of allowing the Holy Spirit to enter into each person.

In this Pentecostal church in Tanzania worshippers sing and pray. They believe that the Spirit of God is alive and among them. ▼

Rites of Passage

Christians want to make sure that the teaching and life of Jesus find a place in the pattern of everyday life. Many of the Churches mark stages in a person's life as they grow. Rites of passage are a way of making sure that Jesus is ever present throughout a believer's life.

Baptism

Baptism is the basic Christian rite. Jesus was baptized; therefore people who become Christians are baptized. Babies are baptized in Roman Catholic, Anglican and Orthodox Churches. The ceremony marks the entry of the new baby into the Christian Church. Godparents make promises on behalf of the infant to ensure that he or she will grow up in the Christian faith. Many Protestant Churches, such as the Baptists, baptize adults only ('believer's baptism') as they think a person should only make such promises themselves.

▲ A Danish priest makes the sign of the cross with water on the baby's forehead marking the entry of the baby into the Christian Church.

Confirmation

In some Churches, baptism is followed in teenage (or adult) years with confirmation. The person confirms the promises made on his or her behalf by godparents. Confirmation is a way of ensuring that the person has full membership of the Christian Church.

▲ A wedding in Peru. After the church ceremony, the married couple walk on sacred land to one side of the church.

Marriage

Marriage takes place in church with the couple making promises to each other before God. In God's presence they commit themselves to each other.

Funerals

In many Western countries, although many people may not be active Christians or attend church, most will have a Christian funeral. A ceremony is held in a church when the soul of the dead person is offered up to God. Funerals may be sad occasions for those who are bereaved but they can also be joyous times because the dead person has been 'called home', and 'gone to live with God'. Friends and relatives should rejoice because through Jesus' life, death and resurrection his followers have the opportunity to triumph over death and to live in God's presence forever.

DEATH

Christians believe that Jesus will come again at the end of the world. There will be a Last Judgement which will decide whether a person's soul goes to heaven or hell. Hell is often shown as a fiery furnace with devils torturing the evil ones, while heaven is a blissful place where people live with God. Some Christians believe that because God is Love, everyone, even the most evil, will be saved.

Christianity Today

Christianity has had 2,000 years of history since the life of Jesus. In the West and in the Americas, Christianity continues to be the major religion. This reflects the spread of the Roman Empire in the first 500 years of Christianity. However, in India and the Far East it has been less successful. The Indian Church traces its origins back to Thomas, one of Jesus' disciples, but in India today only 2 per cent of people are Christian.

▲ A religious parade in Spain. Christian festivals and customs are a major part of Europe's culture.

There has been a rapid rise of Christianity in Africa and China, but fewer people are going to church in Europe. Church-going is still popular in the USA and Central and South America. Only about 5–6 per cent of people attend church regularly in the UK (although over 38 million British people claim to be Christian). However, in parts of the USA 45–50 per cent of people go to church.

During the twentieth century most of the different types of Christianity realized they must work together. In the past, they had often worked against each other, each claiming they understood the life of Jesus better than the other. It was very difficult for would-be Christians to understand why they should join one group rather than another. The World Council of Churches was formed in 1949 to help churches understand each other better and to debate and discuss differences. The word used to describe this co-operation is 'ecumenical' (meaning 'one world'). Churches may continue to have different views but try to work as 'one body' whenever they can.

Christians today still try to put Jesus' teaching into practice in the world. They are willing to put differences to one side. They all want to teach the 'Good News' of Jesus, their Lord and their God, and follow his example.

A humble building serves as a church in Tanzania, Africa.▼

▲ The Roman Catholic Church continues to attract huge congregations in countries such as the Philippines.

CHRISTIANITY – FACTS AND FIGURES

There are over two billion Christians in the world. Half of them are Roman Catholic and, of these, about 500 million live in Central and South America. The majority of Christians today are non-white and live in the southern hemisphere. There are over 22,000 different Christian groups or sects. Christianity is growing fast in Africa: the number of Christians in 1950 was 25 million; by 1980 it was 100 million and by 2000 it was over 200 million.

Glossary

Baptism A ceremony of sprinkling or pouring water on to a person's forehead, or of immersing him or her in water. It symbolizes the joining of the Christian Church.

Baptist A person who baptizes someone. Also, a person who believes only adults should be baptized.

BCE Before Christian Era.

Blasphemy Disrespectful talk about God or sacred things.

CE Christian Era.

Census An official count of people in a country.

Christ The anointed one: often called 'Messiah' from the Hebrew.

Church A Christian organization, or a building used for Christian worship, or all Christians worldwide.

Crucified Put to death by being nailed or bound to a cross.

Devil The supreme spirit of evil. A very wicked or cruel person.

Disciple Someone who followed Jesus during his life. A follower or pupil of a teacher.

Epistles Letters.

Garden of Eden The place given to Adam and Eve, the first people (according to the Bible), to care for. A place which was perfect.

Gentiles The name given to non-Jews by the Jews.

Gospels 'Good News'. The stories of Jesus' life and work.

Holy Concerned with God or religion, 'sacred'.

Hypocrites People who think they are better than other people.

Kingdom of God (Heaven) The place where God rules: a place of peace where people live together with God.

Ministry Work with, and spiritual service to, other people.

Miracles Extraordinary and welcome events that cannot be explained by the laws of nature or science.

Orthodox Churches of Greece and Slavonic countries.

Parables Stories with levels of meanings used to make a point. Jesus used parables in his teaching.

Persecuted Treated very badly over a long time.

Pharisees Members of one of the important Jewish groups at the time of Jesus.

Pilgrims People who travel to a holy place for religious reasons.

Pope The Bishop of Rome; the leader of the Roman Catholic Church.

Prophets People who speak for God and tell people what God wants.

Protestant A member of those Churches separate from the Roman Catholic and Orthodox Churches.

Religious Concerned with or believing in a religion.

Resurrection Jesus' rising from the dead.

Roman Catholic A member of the Church giving loyalty to the Bishop of Rome.

Sabbath The Jewish holy day. It begins before sunset on Friday and ends at nightfall on Saturday.

Sermon A religious talk.

Sin Going against God's wishes.

Soul The spiritual part of a person.

Synagogue A building where Jewish people meet, pray and study.

Temple The focus for the Jews at the time of Jesus. Destroyed in 70 CE by the Romans.

Torah The Five Books of Moses. It can also mean the Jewish Bible or the whole of Jewish law.

Further Information

Books to read

Christians: Through the Ages, Round the World by John Drane (Lion Publishing, 1993)

Festival Tales: Christian Festivals by Saviour Pirotta (Hodder Wayland, 2001)

Jesus and Mary by Graham Owen and Alison Seaman (Wayland, 1998)

The Jesus Story by M Batchelor (Lion Publishing, 1999)

Living Religions: Christianity Part 1 by Clare Richards (Nelson, 1997)

Religions of the World: The Christian World by Alan Brown (Hodder Wayland, 2001)

Stories from the Christian World by David Self (Macdonald Young Books, 1998)

Teaching About Jesus by A Ewens A & M K Stone (RMEP, 2001)

Videos

Quest Life Stories (Channel 4)

StoryKeepers videos (13 episodes) (Paternoster Publishing, www.paternoster-publishing.com)

God's Story – New Testament (Yorkshire Television/Granada Learning)

CD-ROMs

Encyclopaedia of the Bible and Christianity (2nd edition) (Lion Publishing, 1998)

Lion PC Bible Handbook (Lion Publishing, 1997)

Web pages

www.theresite.org.uk
The RE site: 'your starting point for RE on the web'. Index to over 300 RE resources drawn from all over the web.

www.culham.ac.uk
Website of Culham College Institute which promotes good practice in, and awareness of, RE.

www.natsoc.org.uk
Website of National Society (Church of England) for Promoting RE.

www.re-xs.ucsm.ac.uk
RE Exchange Service (linked to National Grid for Learning) with a 'Teachers' Cupboard' resource page.

www.stapleford-centre.org
An independent education centre, focusing on training for teachers.

Other media resources

BBC Education produces schools media resources on different faiths.
BBC Information
PO Box 1116, Belfast BT2 7AJ
Tel: 08700 100 222   email: info@bbc.co.uk
www.bbc.co.uk/schools

Channel 4 produces schools media resources on different faiths, including Animated World Faiths.
C4 Schools
PO Box 100, Warwick CV34 6TZ
Tel: 01926 436444
email: sales@schools.channel4.co.uk
www.channel4.com/schools

The Commonwealth Institute Resource Centre
Kensington High Street, London W8 6NQ
Tel: 0207 603 4535
http://www.commonwealth.org.uk

Index

The numbers in **bold** refer to photographs and maps, as well as text.